*When an emotional injury takes place,
the body begins a process
as natural as the healing
of a physical wound.*

*Trust the process.
Let it happen.
Surrender to it.*

Trust that nature will do the healing.
Know that the pain will pass,
and, when it passes,
you will be stronger,
happier, more sensitive and aware.

This is a book to be <u>used</u>,
not just read.

*If you are experiencing a loss
and are in need of emotional first aid,
please turn directly to page 20.*

The fact that you are
reading these pages
means that you have already
chosen to survive.

Congratulations.

And welcome.

A companion workbook to
How to Survive the Loss of a Love is available.
It's entitled *Surviving, Healing & Growing.*

How to Survive the Loss of a Love
is available on audio tape
—complete and unabridged.

The poetry in this volume was taken from
*Come Love With Me & Be My Life:
The Collected Romantic Poetry
of Peter McWilliams*

All available at your local bookstore, or by calling
1-800-LIFE-101

How to Survive the Loss of a Love

by

Melba Colgrove, Ph.D.,
Harold H. Bloomfield, M.D.,
& Peter McWilliams

ISBN 0-553-07760-0

Published by
Prelude Press
8165 Mannix Drive
Los Angeles, California 90046

Cover Design: Paul LeBus
Desktop Publishing: Sara J. Thomas

Distributed by Bantam Books
Published simultaneously in the United States and Canada

DEDICATION

To All Good.

To my father, whose death when I was four, consti-
tuted a near overwhelming loss.

To my mother, grandparents and all those perceptive
others—then and now—who help me survive,
heal and grow.

To my daughter Bliss; her husband, Joe; and her best
friend, Nancy.

To my other persistent supporters: Peter, Susie, Car-
olyn, Carl, G.S. Khalsa, M.D., Frank Greene,
M.D., both Gay and David Williamson and the
Miesel family.

To all those who refuse for long to remain deadened,
indifferent or uncaring...choosing instead to come
alive again.

—Melba

To my wife Sirah, daughter Shazara, mother Fridl, sis-
ter Nora and dear friend Robert, for their love and
support to help me not only survive but thrive.

To my courageous patients for teaching me about
surviving, healing and growing.

To Maharishi Mahesh Yogi, who brought the Tran-
scendental Meditation program into my life at a
time when I needed it most.

To dear Peter and Melba for their gifts and shared
learning.

To the wonder and joy of it all.

—Harold

For Melba and Joan and Ginny, for Mom, J-R and for
all my fellow survivors.

Thank you!
—Peter

Contents

UNDERSTANDING LOSS

SURVIVING

HEALING

GROWING

To every thing there is a season,
and a time to every purpose
under the heaven.

A time to be born, and a time to die;
a time to plant,
and a time to pluck up that which is planted;

A time to kill, and a time to heal;
a time to break down, and a time to build up;

A time to weep, and a time to laugh;
a time to mourn, and a time to dance;

A time to cast away stones,
and a time to gather stones together;
a time to embrace,
and a time to refrain from embracing;

A time to get, and a time to lose;
a time to keep, and a time to cast away;

A time to rend, and a time to sew;
a time to keep silence, and a time to speak;

A time to love, and a time to hate;
a time of war, and a time of peace.

Ecclesiastes
3:1-8

UNDERSTANDING LOSS

I find
I lost.

If you are experiencing a loss and are in need of emotional first aid, please turn directly to page 20. Return and read these introductory pages when you have time.

Let's take a moment to view loss in the larger perspective. In nature, loss is an essential element of creation—the rose blossoms, the bud is lost; the plant sprouts, the seed is lost; the day begins, the night is lost. In all cases, loss sets the stage for further creation (or, more accurately, re-creation).

So it is in human life. It's hard to look back on any gain in life that does not have a loss attached to it.

With this firmly in mind we can examine the various losses in life. (Without this overview, it tends to become awfully depressing.)

OBVIOUS LOSSES

- —death of a loved one
- —break-up of an affair
- —separation
- —divorce
- —loss of job
- —loss of money
- —robbery
- —rape or other violent crime

NOT-SO-OBVIOUS LOSSES

- —moving
- —illness (loss of health)
- —changing teachers, changing schools
- —success (the loss of striving)
- —loss of a cherished ideal
- —loss of a long-term goal

LOSS RELATED TO AGE

—childhood dreams

—puppy love

—crushes

—adolescent romances

—leaving school (dropping out or graduating)

—leaving home

—loss of "youth"

—loss of "beauty"

—loss of hair or teeth

—loss of sexual drive (or worse, the drive remains but the ability falters)

—menopause

—retirement

LIMBO LOSSES

(Is it on? Is it off? Is it a gain? Is it a loss?)

—awaiting medical tests or reports on their outcome

—a couple on the brink of divorce for the fourteenth time

—a friend, spouse or relative "missing in action"

—lovers, after any quarrel

—a business transaction that may or may not fall through

—a lawsuit

—putting your house up for sale

Limbo losses often feel like this:

My life has fallen down
around me before
—lots of times,
for lots of reasons—
usually other people.

And most of the time
I was fortunate enough
to have a large lump of
that life hit me on the
head and render me numb
to the pain & desolation
that followed.
And I survived.
And I live to love again.

But this,
this slow erosion from below
—or within—
it's me falling down around my life
because you're still in that life
—but not really.
And you're out of that life
—but not quite.

I do all right
alone,
and better
together,
but
I do very poorly
when
semi-
together.

In solitude
I do much,
in love
I do more,
but
in doubt
I only transfer
pain to paper
in gigantic Passion Plays
complete with miracles and martyrs
and crucifixions and resurrections.

Come to stay
or
stay away.

This series of passion poems
is becoming a heavy cross to bare.

The feeling of being "in limbo" is itself a loss. Even if the situation turns out fine (the veteran returns, the lover calls and again professes undying love, etc.), while in doubt that doubt is a loss and should be treated accordingly.

- Realize that "not knowing" may be the worst torture of all.

- When in limbo—and your better instincts tell you there's little hope—it's better to end the situation than to let it drag on and on.

- Call or send in your formal notice of termination and get on with the business of surviving, healing and growing.

To give you up.

God!
What bell of freedom
that rings within me.

No more waiting for
letters
phone calls
post cards
that never came.

No more creative energy
wasted
in letters never mailed.

And, after awhile,

no more insomnia,
no more insanity.

Some more happiness,
some more life.

All it took was giving you up.

And that took quite a bit.

INEVITABLE LOSSES

There are inevitable losses—losses in which death or separation is imminent. When you recognize these in advance, it will help greatly to

• Discuss your situation with the person who is leaving.

• If you are the one who is leaving, talk it over with those who are being left.

• Take part in making the decisions that must be made.

• Let your wishes be known.

OTHER LOSSES

Temporary losses (lover on vacation, spouse in the service, son or daughter away at school, a slump in business)—even when we know the outcome will eventually be positive—are losses nonetheless.

Even success has built into it certain losses—the loss of a goal to strive for and the changes that are almost certainly part of success.

There are also innumerable "mini losses" that tend to add up during the course of a day, week, month or life. An unexpected dent in the car here, an argument with a friend there, and one can find oneself "inexplicably" depressed.

Each of these losses—immediate or cumulative, sudden or eventual, obvious or not—creates an emotional wound, an injury to the organism.

WHAT LOSS FEELS LIKE

Along with the obvious feelings of pain, depression and sadness, there are other reactions to loss, such as

• feeling helpless, fearful, empty, despairing, pessimistic, irritable, angry, guilty, restless

• experiencing a loss of concentration, hope, motivation, energy

• any changes in appetite, sleep patterns or sexual drive

• a tendency to be more fatigued, error-prone and slower in speech and movement

Any or all of these are to be expected during and after a loss. It's part of the body's natural healing process. Be with these changes; don't fight them. It's OK.

If you haven't had an obvious loss, and yet you relate strongly to a good number of these reactions, you may want to examine the recent past to see if a not-so-obvious loss—or a series of them—has taken place.

If so, you might want to follow a few of the suggestions given in this book. Your mind and body are already involved in the healing process.

THE STAGES OF RECOVERY

- Recovering from a loss takes place in three distinct—yet overlapping—stages.

- They are

  —shock/denial/numbness
  —fear/anger/depression
  —understanding/acceptance/moving on

- Each stage of recovery is

  —necessary
  —natural
  —a part of the healing process

the fear that I would
come home one day and
find you gone has turned
into the pain of the
reality.

"What will I do if it happens?"
I would ask myself.

What will I do
now that it
has?

The first stage of recovery is **shock/denial/ numbness.**

- We cannot believe or comprehend what has happened to us.

- The mind denies the loss.

- Often the first words uttered after hearing of a loss are, "What?" or "Oh, no."

- We forget that a loss has taken place, and find ourselves stunned each time we remember again. (This is especially true after awakening from sleep.)

- Meanwhile, the body's natural protection against intense pain—shock and numbness— is activated.

morning.
we wake & snuggle.

afternoon.
a phone call, california beckons.

evening.
the airport, a brutal good(?)bye.

night.
o my god. o my god. o my god.

mourning. again.

I know it was time for us
to part,

but today?

I know I had much pain to
go through,

but tonight

?

The second stage of recovery is **fear/anger/depression.**

- Fear, anger and depression are emotions and reactions most often associated with loss.

> rain.
> it
> rained.
> I
> fell.
> it
> rained.
> I
> loved.
> it
> rained.
> I
> lost.
> it
> rained.
> It
> loved.
> I
> rained.
> rain.

What do I do
now that you're gone?

Well, when there's
nothing else going on,
which is quite often,
I sit in a corner and
I cry
until I am
too numbed
to feel.

Paralyzed, motionless
for awhile, nothing
moving
inside or out.

Then I think
how much I miss you.

Then I feel
fear
pain
loneliness
desolation.

Then
I cry
until I am
too numbed
to feel.

Interesting pastime.

And finally, **understanding/acceptance/moving on**.

- We have survived.
- Our body is well on the way to healing.
- Our mind accepts that life without what was lost is possible.
- We move on to a new chapter of our life.

the sun will rise
in a few minutes.

it's been doing it
—regularly—
for as long as I
can remember.

maybe I should
pin my hopes
on important,
but often
unnoticed,
certainties
like that,

not on such relatively
trivial matters as
whether you will ever
love me.
or not.

I must conquer my loneliness

alone.

I must be happy with myself
or I have
nothing
to offer.

Two halves have
little choice
but to
join,
and yes,
they do
make a
whole.

but two
wholes,
when they coincide...

that is
beauty.

that is
love.

- We go through the three stages of recovery no matter what we lose.

- Loss is loss, no matter what the cause. When someone or something we love is taken from us or denied us, that is a loss.

- The only difference in recovering from one loss or another is the *intensity* of feeling and the *duration* of the healing process.

- The greater our loss,

  —the more intensely we feel each of the stages of recovery

  —the longer it takes to pass from one stage to another

- With small losses, the three stages of recovery can be moved through in minutes. For large losses, it can take years.

- The body, mind and emotions have enormous wisdom. They know how to heal themselves, and the amount of time they will need to do it.

- Give them what they need to heal.

- Trust in the process of recovery.

SURVIVING

Thursday:
drowning in love

Friday:
drowning in doubt

Saturday:
drowning

Sunday:
God, I can't drag my
self to church this morning.
Please make a house call.

One:
You Will Survive

- You *will* get better.

- No doubt about it.

- The healing process has a beginning, a middle and an end.

- Keep in mind, at the beginning, that there *is* an end. It's not that far off. You *will* heal.

- Nature is on your side, and nature is a powerful ally.

- Tell yourself, often, "I am alive. I will survive."

- You are alive.

- You will survive.

in my sleep
I dreamed
you called. you said
you were moving back
with your old lover.
you said you thought a
phone call would be the
cleanest way to handle it,
"it" being that we could
never see each other
again, and that I should
understand why.
I moved to wake
myself and found I wasn't
sleeping after all.
my life became
a nightmare.

Two:
If You Need It,
Get Help at Once

- If you think you need help, don't hesitate. Get it at once.

- If you are feeling suicidal—or even think you *might* be feeling suicidal—call a Suicide Prevention Hotline *at once.*

- To find the number, call Directory Assistance and ask for "The Suicide Prevention Hotline." Almost every town has one. (And notice how *nice* the directory assistance operator suddenly becomes.) (Our thoughts on suicide are on page 68.)

- You should also seek help *at once* if you...

  —feel you are "coming apart"

  —are no longer in control

  —are about to take an action you may later regret

  —have a history of emotional disturbance

  —turn to alcohol, drugs or other addictive substances in time of need

  —feel isolated with no one to turn to

  —repeatedly find yourself in loss situations

- Help can be found in—of all places—the Yellow Pages. Explore the organizations under such listings as "Help Lines."

- This is not the time to "be brave" and attempt to "go it alone." In fact, it takes great courage to ask for help.

I found
in you
a home.

Your departure
left me a
Shelterless Victim
of a
Major Disaster.

I called the
Red Cross,
but they
refused to
send over
a nurse.

Three:
Acknowledge the Loss

- You may struggle to both believe and disbelieve that this could have happened to you.

- It has happened. It is real.

- Recognize that a loss has taken place.

- You may wonder if you are strong enough to bear such a loss.

- You are strong enough.

- You are alive.

- You will survive.

*there is nothing to be
done.*

only accept it…

and hurt.

Four:
You Are Not Alone

- Loss is a part of life, of being alive, of being human.

- Everyone experiences loss.

- Everyone.

- Your task is to make the journey from immediate loss to eventual gain as rapidly, smoothly and courageously as possible.

- Somehow, the camaraderie of mutual suffering eases the pain.

- You have comrades—almost six billion on this planet alone.

Our love affair
has crash landed.

I am trapped
in the rubble
of gossamer wings.

The Wright brothers
would have been proud
of our flight, but
we live in an age
of moon landings and
space shuttles.
Our flight was pitifully low
and painfully brief.

Endings
make the circumstances
of the beginnings
regrettable.

Five:
It's OK to Feel

- It's OK to feel numb. Expect to be in shock for awhile. This emotional numbness may be frightening.

- It's OK to feel fear. "Will I make it?" "Will I ever love again?" "Will I ever feel good about anything again?" These are familiar fears that follow a loss. It's OK to *feel* them, but, to the degree you can, don't *believe* them.

- It's OK to feel nothing. There are times when you'll have no feelings of any kind. That's fine.

- It's OK to feel anything. You may feel grief-stricken, angry, like a failure, exhausted, muddled, lost, beaten, indecisive, relieved, overwhelmed, inferior, melancholy, giddy, silly, loathful, full of self-hatred, envious, suicidal (*feeling* suicidal is OK; acting upon the feeling is not), disgusted, happy, outraged, in rage or *anything else*.

- *All* feelings are part of the healing process.

- Let yourself feel. Let yourself heal.

Spring:
leaves grow.
love grows.

Summer:
love dies.
I drive away,
tears in my eyes.

Bugs commit suicide on my windshield.

Autumn:
leaves fall.
I fall.

Winter:
I die.
I drive away,
nothing in my eyes.

Snowflakes commit suicide on my windshield.

Six:
Be with the Pain

- If you're hurting, admit it.

- To feel pain after loss is

    —normal

    —natural

    —proof that you are alive

    —a sign that you are able to respond to life's experiences

- Although you may be frightened by it, be with your pain. Feel it. Lean into it. You will not find it bottomless.

- It is an important part of the healing process that you be with the pain, experience the desolation, feel the hurt.

- Don't deny it or cover it or run away from it. Be with it. Hurt for a while.

- See pain as not hurting, but as healing.

you came
and made
my house
our home

you left
making
our home
my asylum

Seven:
You're Great!

- You are a good, whole, worthwhile human being.

- You are OK. You are more than OK, you're *great*.

- Your self-esteem may have suffered a jolt. Your thoughts may reflect some guilt, worry, condemnation or self-deprecation. These thoughts are just symptoms of the stress you are going through.

- There is no need to give negative thoughts about yourself the center of your attention.

- Don't punish yourself with "if only's." ("*If only* I had [or hadn't] done this [or that], I wouldn't be in this emotional mess.") Disregard any thought that begins "If only..."

- You are much more than the emotional wound you are currently suffering. Don't lose sight of that.

- Beneath the surface turmoil

   —you are good
   —you are whole
   —you are beautiful

  just because you are.

I am Joy.
I am everything.
I can do all things but two:

1. forget that I love you.

2. forget that you no longer love me.

Eight:
Give Yourself Time to Heal

- The healing process takes time.

- The greater the loss, the more time it will take to heal.

- In this age of fast foods and instantly replace-able everything, it's hard to accept that any-thing takes time.

- You require time to heal. Give yourself the luxury of that time.

- You deserve it.

Pain
is not so heavy
a burden in
summer.

Walks
through
travelogue scenes
prevent a good
deal of destruction.

And,
even though no one
is there to warm me,
the sun will.

But
Fall just fell,
leaving Winter,
and me,
with no
warmth within
to face
the cold without.

I might just stick
to the sidewalk
and freeze.

Nine:
The Healing Process
Has Its Progressions
and Regressions

- The process of healing and growth is not the smooth progression many people assume.

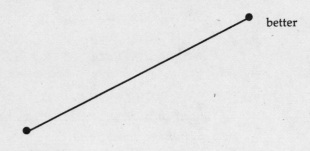

better

not so better

- It's more like a lightning bolt, full of ups and downs, progressions and regressions, dramatic leaps and depressing backslides.

better

not so better

- Realize this and know that whether you are "better" or "worse" than yesterday—or five minutes ago—the healing process is under way.

life is becoming.
less livable.

with each new person I meet
I wonder, is this the day
fate has chosen, or is fate
what I have chosen to get me
through the day?

loving
is the most
creative
force of the universe.

the memory of loving,
the most
destructive.

Ten:
Tomorrow Will Come

- Life contains many positive experiences.
- The good is on its way.
- No doubt about it, tomorrow will come.

First,
I have to get
out
of love with you.

Second,
I have to remember:

don't fall
until you see
the whites
of their
lies.

Eleven:
Breathe!

- Take a breath, deep into your lower abdomen.

- Breathing is healing.

- Breathing is life.

- Exhale fully. Take another slow, deep breath.

- Use the breath to stretch your abdomen, stomach and chest.

- Place your hand on your heart, stomach or any other part of your body that seems to be in turmoil. Breathe into that area. Tell yourself

    —"Peace. Be still."

    —"I am alive. I will survive."

this longing
may shorten
my life.

Twelve:
Get Lots of Rest—Now

- Rest.

- Sleep more.

- Obtain help with ongoing tasks.

- Arrange your life so that you get lots of rest. Schedule rest into the day. Plan to go to bed earlier and sleep a bit later.

- Be gentle with yourself. Don't rush about. Your body needs energy for repair.

- Meditate.

- Rest your emotions. Don't become "heavily involved" for awhile.

- Productive work often helps rest the emotions. Do as much of that as is comfortable.

- Rest is the foundation of health.

*(there is no poem
on this page
as the poet
decided to
take a nap)*

Thirteen:
Stick to Your Schedule

- OK, enough rest. Get going!

- Alternating rest with activity brings efficient healing.

- Rest as much as you need to, but don't become lethargic. Keep active.

- While your inner world is chaotic, maintain a modified (lightened) schedule in the outer. This gives you a sense of order—also something to hold onto.

Although my
nature is not to
live by day,

I cannot
tolerate another
night like this.

So,

I will wake up
early
tomorrow morning and
do do do
all day long,

falling asleep
exhausted tomorrow
early evening,
too tired
even for
nightmares.

Fourteen:
Keep Decision-Making to a Minimum

- Expect your judgement to be clouded.

- Keep decision-making to a minimum.

- Postpone major decisions, if possible.

- Ask friends, family and business associates to make minor decisions for you.

- Delegate; relegate; rest.

- Too much change has already taken place—that's why you're hurting. Keep additional changes to a minimum.

Plans:

Next month:
find something new.

This month:
get over you.

This week:
get you back.

Today:
survive.

Fifteen:
It's OK to Make "Silly" Mistakes

- You may forget your keys, misplace your wallet, drop a glass or misspell your own name—several times in a row.

- Absentmindedness, forgetfulness and clumsiness are frequently experienced after a loss.

- It's a variation on walking into a room to get something, and forgetting what it was you went to get—except that after a loss it's worse, and more frequent.

- It's OK. Be easy with yourself. You're healing. If you have any reaction to the silliness of your mistakes, let it be one of amusement rather than irritation.

something's
wrong.

Sixteen:
It's OK to Go through the Motions in Slow Motion

- You may go through your activities as though you were surrounded by warm Jello.

- Your arms and legs may feel heavy. You may lean on things to support the weight of your body. It may even be difficult to hold up your head.

- Your speech may be slurred or slowed.

- You may feel as though you're in a trance.

- All of this can be frightening.

- Know, however, that all this is part of the process of healing. The body slows its outer motions to provide the energy necessary for inner healing.

- Don't push yourself. Relax. For a while, go slow.

I remember thinking once
that it would be good
if you left because
then I could get some
Important Things
done.

Since you've left I've done
nothing. nothing
is as important
as you.

Seventeen:
It's OK to Need Comforting

- It's OK to be taken care of for awhile.

- Accept understanding and support from
    - —friends
    - —family
    - —co-workers

- An emotional wound is real, debilitating and painful. It's OK to need comfort.

- Some people are so good at comforting that they do it professionally. Feel free to seek the help of a health care professional with whom you feel comfortable.

- Be brave enough to accept the help of others.

My friends are still here:

neglected,
rejected
while I gave all my
precious moments to
you.

They're still here!

God bless them.

Eighteen:
Seek the Support of Others

- Although you may be afraid to do so, ask others for help. It's a human (and courageous) thing to do.

- Gather your friends, family and co-workers into a support system. You need to know that others care, and, if you tell them your pain, they will help.

- The telephone is a marvelous tool for support. Use it. Call friends, family, help lines.

- Invite a friend to stay overnight.

- Visit a relative (preferably at dinnertime).

- Neighbors can be wonderful.

- Strangers are merely friends you haven't yet met.

help me up
my friend.

dust me off.

feed me warmth.

you are comfort.

let me lean on you
until I can stand
alone.

I will stand a little taller then,

and you will be
proud
to have a friend
such as me.

Nineteen:
Touching and Hugging

- The healing power of touch cannot be over-estimated.

- If someone asks, "What can I do?" perhaps all you need to say is, "Hold my hand" or "Give me a hug."

- Get three hugs a day for survival, five for maintenance and eight (or more!) for growth.

- When others are not available to hug you—hug yourself. Go ahead. It feels good.

- Now's a great time for a nurturing massage.

- The most healing touch may be gently caressing yourself. If a part of you hurts, touch it and tell it, "I am here for you. I love you."

*One
touch
is worth
ten thousand
words.*

Twenty:
Find Others Who Have
Survived a Similar Loss

- The support of others who *know* what you're going through can be invaluable.

- Your friends may know someone who has survived a similar loss.

- There are many organizations dedicated to serving those with specific losses. Look in your local Yellow Pages under "Social Service Organizations" or "Human Service Organizations."

- People who have survived similar losses can provide support, guidance—and are proof that you too will survive.

all the goodness
of my life is
gone.

first you,
and with you
joy
love
freedom.

then
colors
music
trees.

even creativity,
which is always
the last to go,
is only making
a token appearance.

Twenty-one:
Seek Wise Guidance

- Wisdom has three components: love, firmness and knowledge. Look for these traits in those from whom you seek and accept guidance.

- Wise people can help you in fulfilling your schedule of tasks. You may need someone to "walk you through" your day.

- You can often find such people in your church, office, family, 12-step or other self-help groups.

- Beware, however, of anyone's well-meaning advice containing

    —should

    —you better

    —it's time you

    —I think you should

- Such approaches, far from being supportive, only foster guilt and a sense of inadequacy.

Excuse me.

I am currently
afflicted with the world's
number one crippler:
infatuation fixation paralysis,

commonly referred to as
love.

Any spare comfort
you have to give
would be most appreciated,
although my ability to receive
may be temporally impaired.

Thank you.

Twenty-two:
Surround Yourself with Things That Are Alive

- Don't isolate yourself from life.

- In addition to family and friends, invite other living things into your life:

    —a new plant

    —a stray kitten

    —the puppy you've always wanted

    —a bowl of goldfish

    —even a bowl of fresh fruit has its own joy and consolation to offer. (And then you can eat it.)

I'd have a nervous breakdown,
only
I've been through
this too many
times to be
nervous.

Twenty-three:
Reaffirm Your Beliefs

- Reaffirm any beliefs in which you have faith or have found useful in the past.

- These may include religious, spiritual, psychological or philosophical beliefs you find appealing and valuable.

- Use any body of knowledge you find comforting, inspiring or uplifting.

- Reexplore it, lean on it, grow from it, enjoy it.

Missing your love
with God's so
close at hand.

It seems somehow
a sacrilege...

but I think
He understands.

Twenty-four:
Sundays Are the Worst

- No doubt about it.

- Holidays are the second-worst.

- Saturday nights aren't much fun, either.

- The feelings of separation may feel greater than usual three days, three weeks, three months, six months and a year after the loss.

- Schedule particularly comforting activities into these periods of time.

Yesterday was Sunday.
Sundays are always bad.
("Bloody," as they have been aptly described.)

The full moon is Wednesday.
Full moons are always bad.
(Ask Lon Chaney.)

Friday is Good Friday
and, 30 miles from Rome,
the vibrations of all those mourning
worshippers will make it bad.

Sunday is Easter—but it's also
Sunday,
and Sundays are always bad.

Twenty-five:
The Question of Suicide

- You may be having suicidal thoughts. They may or may not be as eloquent as *"to be or not to be,"* but they may arise.

- Know they are a natural symptom of the pain, and that there is no need to act on them.

- If you fear these impulses are getting out of hand, seek professional help *at once.* Call directory assistance and ask for the number of your local Suicide Prevention Hotline. Then call it. The people (almost entirely volunteers) are there to help. They *want* to help. Give them the gift of allowing them to do so.

- Don't turn the rage you feel against yourself. (Although feeling rage is perfectly all right—after all, an utterly outrageous thing has happened to you.) Find a safe way to release it. Beat a pillow, cry, scream, stomp up and down, yell.

- Above all, suicide is silly. It's leaving the World Series ten minutes into the first inning just because your favorite hitter struck out. It's walking out of the opera during the overture just because the conductor dropped his baton. It's...well, you get the picture. In this play called life, aren't you even a *little* curious about what might happen next?

- The feeling *will pass.* You can count on that. You *will* get better. *Much* better.

- We *do* promise you a rose garden. We just can't promise you it will be totally without thorns.

THE QUESTION OF SUICIDE:

Keep it a question.
It's not really an answer.

HEALING

one thing I forgot:

after the
pain of parting
comes the
happiness of healing;

rediscovering
life,
friends,
self.

Joy.

Twenty-six:
Do Your Mourning Now

- Don't postpone, deny, cover or run from your pain. Be with it. Now.

- Everything else can wait. An emotional wound requires the same priority treatment as a physical wound. Set time aside to mourn.

- The sooner you allow yourself to be with your pain, the sooner it will pass. The only way *out* is *through*.

- When you resist mourning, you interfere with the body's natural stages of recovery.

- If you postpone the healing process, grief can return months—even years—later to haunt you.

- Feel the fear, pain, desolation, anger. It's essential to the healing process.

- You are alive. You will survive.

Grief is a quiet thing.
Deadly in repose.
A raging horror, a thunder of abuse.

Raucous—
Demanding—
Incomprehensible—
Tearing all that one has ever loved.

Hopeless,
Forlorn,
Fear-ridden and misunderstood;
Ceasing a moment, and through the years
Returning...to destroy.

To rage,
To curse all that is happy—
or contented,
or trusting.

To threaten every beauty that is true.

Grief?
It's a quiet thing.

—Melba Colgrove

Twenty-seven:
Earlier Losses May Surface

- You may have unresolved losses from the past: previous relationships, rejections, disappointments, hurts—and that wellspring of loss: childhood.

- A contemporary loss can reactivate a prior, unhealed loss.

- You may feel that you're responding "unreasonably" to a loss. In fact, you may be healing past losses, too.

- Give yourself permission to mend it all.

- Let it heal.

- A great book for *Making Peace with Your Parents* is by Harold H. Bloomfield, M.D. with Leonard Felder, Ph.D. Available at your local bookstore.

*I sat evaluating
myself.*

*I decided
to lie down.*

Twenty-eight:
Be Gentle with Yourself

- Be *very* gentle with yourself—kind, forgiving, tender.

- Accept that you have an emotional wound, that it is debilitating, and that it will take awhile before you are completely well.

- Treat yourself with the same care and affection you would a good friend in a similar situation.

- Don't take on new responsibilities. If appropriate, let your coworkers and employer know you've suffered a loss and are healing.

- Avoid situations in which you may be stressed, challenged or upset.

- Accept assistance and support when offered, but remember that care and compassion begin at home—from yourself to yourself.

- And, for heaven sakes (and your own), don't blame yourself for any "mistakes" (either real or imagined) you think you may have made that brought you to this loss.

- You're great!

To lose you as a
love
was painful.

To lose you as a
friend
is equally painful.

But lost you are.

The walls are sooo high,
and that finely honed saber
I had when I began storming
your citadel isn't even
sharp enough to
slash my wrists.

It's not that I don't care.

It's just that I can't
let myself
care any more.

Twenty-nine:
Heal at Your Own Pace

- Although others may demand it, don't feel the need to immediately "understand" why the loss happened, or instantly "accept" the loss gracefully.

- They'll tell you to "shrug it off," "roll with the punches" and "snap out of it."

- If you succumb to such pressure and superficially dismiss your loss with such popular phrases as
    - —"That's life"
    - —"Oh, well"
    - —"It doesn't matter"
    - —"Who cares?"

  your artificial "acceptance" may interfere with healing.

- Healing is a process. You have the full right to experience the process in your own way, to gain *your* understandings and realizations in your own time.

- To demanding friends, you can quote the proverb: "Be patient. God (or nature) hasn't finished healing me yet."

- Be patient with impatient friends.

This season is called
fall
because everything
nature builds
all summer long
falls
apart.

Like our love.

Thirty:
Don't Try to Rekindle the Old Relationship

- Futile attempts at reconciliation are

    —painful
    —anti-healing
    —anti-growth
    —a waste of valuable energy
    —stupid
    —irresistible

- Resist. To give up this final hope may be the most difficult challenge of all.

- Invest your energies in healing and growing, in yourself, in new relationships and in life.

- Learning to let go can be one of life's greatest lessons.

The layers I have put
around the pain of
your going are thin.

I walk softly through
life, adding thickness
each day.

A thought or a feeling
of you cracks the surface.

A call to you
shatters it all.

And I spend that night in death,

spinning the first
layer of life
with the sunrise.

Thirty-one:
Make a Pact with a Friend

- If the urge to contact the "long lost love" is strong, make a pact—a contract—with a friend.

- Don't make the pact unreasonable. An example of an unreasonable pact might be, "I will never see him/her as long as I live!"

- A more reasonable pact is, "Before I contact him/her, I will contact you first and talk about it."

- Sometimes the support of another can get you through those "irresistible periods," and keep you from doing something you know you'll probably regret later.

*She asked me if seeing
you was a drain.*

Seeing you is not a drain.

It's a sewer.

Thirty-two:
Mementos

- If you find photographs and mementos help-ful in the mourning process, use them.

- If you find mementos bind you to a dead past, get rid of them—put them in the attic, sell them, give them away or throw them out.

- Don't make any "thing" more important than your healing—or yourself.

*I ceremoniously disposed
of all the objects
connected with you.
I thought they were
contaminated.
It did not help.*

I'm the one that's contaminated!

Thirty-three:
Anticipate a Positive Outcome

- Whatever you pay attention to—focus upon—becomes more powerful in your life.

- Focus on a positive outcome. Expect it. Anticipate it. Plan on it.

- It *will* come.

- Be with the sadness, fear and pain when it comes, but don't dwell on it. Accept it, but don't invite it (except during your scheduled periods of mourning).

- Pain is an acceptable guest, but it is not a welcome long-term visitor.

How will it happen?
How will it happen
when I find some
someone to spend
a goodly portion
of my life with?

It must.
I mean, I've been
pre-pairing
so long...

It will happen.
Yes.

I will not dwell on
if, only
how, when, where, whom.

Thirty-four:
Expect to Feel Afraid

- Fear is a natural result of loss, a part of the healing process.

- There are so many things to fear when one suffers a loss:

  —fear of being alone

  —fear of being deserted or rejected

  —fear that you'll never love again

  —fear you'll never be loved again

  —fear of the pain, desolation and torment that may lie ahead

- Far from being the dark thing we are trained to treat fear as a child, fear is, in fact, extra energy to successfully meet the challenges of healing and growing ahead.

- You *will* successfully meet the challenges.

- Fear, when used as the energy it is, can help you meet those challenges.

- Don't fight the fear—use it. Fear is a friend, not an enemy. (More on fear as a friend on page 184.)

as the
memory
of your
light fades
my days grow dark.

my nights are lit with
electric bulbs. I cannot
sleep. I am afraid of the
dark. I am afraid that you
will return and then fade
again. I am afraid that you
will never return. I am
afraid that my next thought
will be of you. I am afraid
that I will run out of poems
before I run out of pain.

Thirty-five:
It's OK to Feel Depressed

- Pretending to have more energy, enthusiasm or happiness than you actually have is not productive. Pretending expends energy that could better be used for healing.

- It's OK to feel "low" for awhile.

- Crying has its own specialness; a cleansing, purifying release.

to those
who ever
wished
me ill:

this night
your wish
has been
fulfilled.

Thirty-six:
It's OK to Feel Anger

* Everyone gets angry at the loss of love. Everyone.

* It's OK to feel anger.

* It's OK to feel anger toward

    —the person who left (even if he or she left you through death)
    —the person who took something or someone away
    —the social conventions or customs that contributed to the loss
    —the fates

* It's *not* OK to

    —hate yourself
    —act upon your anger in a destructive way

* Let the anger out (safely, please!):

    —Hit a pillow.
    —Kick on a bed.
    —Yell and scream (a car parked in a deserted place makes a great "scream chamber").
    —Play volleyball, tennis, handball, soccer.
    —Hit a punching bag.
    —Play piano at full crescendo.

* If the anger is channeled and dissipated in these harmless (indeed, helpful) ways, you'll avoid senseless arguments, accidents and illness.

* Your anger will pass as your hurting heals.

I'm past the point of going
quietly insane.

I'm getting quite
noisy about it.

The neighbors must think
I'm mad.

The neighbors, for once,
think right.

Thirty-seven:
It's OK to Feel Guilty

- When you feel guilty, you are feeling angry with yourself. You violated a belief you have about the way you "should" think, act or feel, and you are mad at yourself for doing so.

- It's OK to feel guilt, but there are limits.

- Just as it's OK to feel anger, but it's *not* OK to hurt someone physically, it's OK to feel angry with yourself, but *not* to the point of illness or incapacity.

- Some regrets are natural, but excessive self-punishment can be harmful.

- The antidote to guilt is forgiveness.

- You may be treating yourself far worse than the loss ever did.

- Don't do that.

- Treat yourself with love, respect, kindness and forgiveness.

*How I
love you and hate you.*

*How bound I am to you.
How bound I am to break my bondage.*

I want to be free!

*I want to be able to
enjoy the day again,*

and give me back my nights.

Thirty-eight:
You May Want to Hire a Professional or Two

- There are many people who, as a profession, help others heal and grow.

- These include (listed here in alphabetical order so as not to slight anyone!)

  —alcohol and substance abuse counselors

  —chiropractors

  —clinical psychologists

  —exercise and fitness trainers

  —homeopaths

  —licensed hypnotherapists

  —marriage, child and family counselors

  —massage therapists

  —medical doctors and other health practitioners

  —nurse practitioners

  —nutritionists

  —pastoral counselors

  —psychiatrists

  —social workers

  —stress management counselors

- If you feel drawn to one or more of these, give them a try. See what the results are. If not helpful, try someone else. If helpful, try him or her again.

all I need is
someone to
talk to
about
you
but
you
are the
only person
I can really
talk to.
trapped.

Thirty-nine:
When You Might Want
Counseling or Therapy

- Most loss, emotional crises or life difficulties do not require psychotherapy.

- Nevertheless, professional assitance may be necessary or useful in the following instances:
    - —if you fear actually doing damage to someone else or yourself—including acting on suicidal thoughts
    - —if you seek solace in alcohol, drugs, overeating or other potentially harmful activities
    - —if the support of wise friends and family is not enough
    - —if you repeatedly find yourself in loss situations
    - —if you don't feel good about yourself, are perpetually out of control or under strain most of the time

- Most people spend more time selecting a car than a therapist. As with any "important purchase," shop around.

- Interview several therapists. Ask questions. What is their method of working with clients? What do they charge? What is their estimated length of treatment?

- How you feel about the therapist is of primary importance. Do you feel comfortable telling her anything about your life? Do you like him? Do you trust her? Does he treat you as an equal? Would you choose this person for a friend?

- With a good therapist, significant benefits can often come in just a few sessions.

As soon as I
became aware
of my
addictive personality,
I gave up drugs
(illegal ones),
and I never started
on the legal poisons
like alcohol
or tobacco
or television.

But, fool that I am,
I forgot to give up
the most addictive
thing around—
The Hard Stuff:
Love.

And now it's too late.

I'm hooked for life.

An emotion-mainliner.
A touch-junkie.

A love addict.

Forty:
A Complete Medical Workup
May Be in Order

- You might want to get a complete medical workup (physical exam, blood tests, the works). It's probably long overdue, anyway.

- There are some physical illnesses triggered by loss, and there are some physical illnesses that *feel* like loss, even though the cause is physical.

- Now might be a good time to take a look at the functioning of your body.

- Your health care provider can best advise you on the value of this suggestion, as well as the extent of the tests.

- If there is anything you fear you *might* discover in these tests, remember that knowledge is better (and more powerful) than fear.

is
romanticism
a
treatable
dis-
ease?

Forty-one:
Some Depressions May Require Medication

• If your symptoms of depression (page 9) seem severe or continue longer than normal, an hour spent with a well-informed psychiatrist discussing your situation and evaluating your next course of action—including the option of medication—can be invaluable.

• All too often, people suffering symptoms of severe depression fail to seek psychiatric treatment because they fear the stigma of "mental illness."

• This is an unfortunate irony because severe, chronic depression is a prevalent and well-recognized medical disorder, one as treatable as diabetes or hypertension.

• Severe biological depression results from a biochemical imbalance in the brain. Antidepressants, taken as prescribed by a psychiatrist, are non-addictive and effective.

• If you wonder whether you need antidepressant medication, contact a competent psychiatrist for an evaluation.

*How many more times will
tears be my only comfort?*

*How many times will I see
that the potential is dead,
and that "our" love was
really in my head?*

*How many more times will
I give up,*

*and how many times will I
want you so bad that nothing
seems good?*

*How many times with you?
How many times
with how many
others?*

Forty-two:
Nutrition

- Giving your body what it needs to function properly—and avoiding the things that interfere with its functioning—is important anytime, but particularly important following a loss.

- Drink lots of water—eight to ten glasses per day.

- Eat more fresh fruits and vegetables. Eat them raw, or lightly steamed.

- Complex carbohydrates (whole grains, potatoes, pasta—yes, pasta!) are excellent sources of nutrition.

- Reduce your intake of caffeine, nicotine, alcohol and cyclamates.

- Beware of junk food attacks and sugar binges!

- Take a good multi-vitamin/mineral supplement. Especially valuable during loss are vitamin C, the B vitamins, calcium and potassium.

- Make all dietary changes *gradually*. Don't jump on a fad-diet bandwagon. Make a few changes, see how you feel, and make a few more.

- Listen to your body. It will tell you what it needs.

The garden loves the rain
and, yes, this is love.

But the love I want for you
—the love I want to give you—
is the love
the rain
gives
the garden.

Loving is giving freedom.

Forty-three:
Remember: You're Vulnerable

- In these days of stress and recovery, remember that you're vulnerable.

- Guard your physical health:

    —Get rest.

    —Don't overextend yourself.

    —Eat sensibly.

    —Get moderate exercise.

    —Drive more carefully.

- Guard your emotional and mental health:

    —Be kind to yourself.

    —Stay away from toxic things, situations and people.

    —Take your time.

    —Don't try to understand, comprehend or figure everything out.

    —Don't take on jobs that aren't yours. (As the Talmud pointed out, "The sun will set without thy assistance.")

- Don't enter into situations in which you must be "convinced." Your sales resistance may be low. Keep that in mind.

- Invite help from people who are trustworthy and able to do what you request of them.

- There is no need to overprotect yourself. Just be aware that much of your energy is being used for healing and that the body's natural defense mechanisms may be weakened.

Once upon a time,
and a very long time
ago it was, too,
I was innocent.

I did not know
what love was.

Pain was when you
fell from a tree.

Forty-four:
Beware of the Rebound

- Nature abhors a vacuum. You may find yourself rushing prematurely into romantic attachments in an attempt to fill that emptiness.

- If your healing isn't complete, an initial rebound is likely to be followed by another loss, a second rebound, another loss, then another, until your emotional life is lived in the ricochet pattern of a handball court.

- Falling "madly in love" soon after a traumatic breakup seems great at first: your wildest hopes and fantasies come true! But then the bottom falls out. You discover the new love is *not* that totally sensuous, intelligent, considerate, understanding, sophisticated god/goddess you initially perceived. Only a human, just like everyone else. Sigh.

- If you want to fall in love with someone, how about trying yourself?

It's always
you & you & you
but it's really
me.

I'll try again
and gain again
and die again
and push on into the night.

To be reborn by a
look and a touch.
And to hope again that
this time it will last,
and to know
it will not be the last.

Forty-five:
Under-Indulge in Addictive Activities

- Beware of anything you may be—or may become—addicted to. *Under*-indulgence in the escape mechanisms of society is in order. *Be with the pain, don't run away from it.*

- Alcohol may numb the pain momentarily, but it is a depressant, and the eventual effect will be greater depression.

- Drugs (marijuana, uppers, downers, all the recreational chemicals) interfere with the natural healing process and should be avoided. A series of momentary "highs" is a poor trade-off for a deepening depression.

- Calorie junkies beware! You may tend to overeat during this time, allowing "unwanted inches" to creep onto your waistline, causing a lowered self-image, resulting in even more depression. Better visit a diet center or your physician instead.

- Smoking more now but enjoying it less?

- Two great books on overcoming the addiction of negative thinking (or any other addiction) are *You Can't Afford the Luxury of a Negative Thought* and its companion workbook *Focus on the Positive* by John-Roger and our own Peter McWilliams. You can find them at your local bookstore, or by calling 1-800-LIFE-101.

I have done it to me again.

*No other being has the power
to hurt me as deeply as I do.*

It is the "need"

The "need" for love.

*I need love because
I am not happy with I;
me is not satisfied with me.*

*In order to stop this hurting
I must reach a point of
contentment within myself.*

*And that'll take
some reaching.*

Forty-six:
Pamper Yourself

- If you have a broken leg and are hospitalized, friends bring you flowers, relatives send baskets of fruit, you lie in bed all day reading or watching TV, nurses give you back rubs, doctors poke, prod and nod encouragingly.

- In short, you are pampered.

- If you have a broken heart, friends expect you to be your cheerful old self, relatives expect you to fulfill all your family obligations and you are expected to show up for work as energetic and efficient as ever.

- In short, you must deal with a world that does not accept the fact that emotional pain not only hurts, but that it can be debilitating.

- The solution? Pamper yourself.

- In addition to the suggestions on the following page, do for yourself whatever your parents did to comfort you as a child.

- Suggestions for pampering yourself:
  - —Take a hot bath (no matter how you feel, thirty minutes after taking a hot bath you'll feel a lot better).
  - —Give or get a massage (rough and vigorous or slow and sensual).
  - —Snack on hot milk and cookies before bed.
  - —Buy yourself something you'd really enjoy.
  - —Treat yourself to your favorite double-dip ice-cream cone (with sprinkles).
  - —Get a manicure, pedicure or any other cure.
  - —Take a trip.
  - —Bask in the sun.
  - —Read a good book.
  - —Watch a good video.
  - —Take time for yourself.
  - —Buy yourself a cashmere anything.
  - —Go to a fine restaurant.
  - —See a good movie, play, opera, horse race.
  - —Visit an art museum.
  - —Buy yourself a bouquet of flowers.
  - —Acquiesce to your whims.
  - —Enjoy!

Forty-seven:
Dreams Can Be Healing

- Healing is a full-time process, 24-hours a day, even while you sleep. Some say *especially* while you sleep.

- You may get messages, information, insights or lessons from your dreams. Be open to them. You may want to keep a notebook by your bed to write them down.

- Nightmares can be the body's process of re-solving issues too painful or disturbing to en-counter consciously. Know that healing is taking place. Once you know the images in a nightmare cannot hurt you, you can watch them like a movie—a horror movie, perhaps, but a movie nonetheless.

- Consciously surround yourself with Goodness and Light before going to sleep, knowing that only that which is for your highest good will take place—no matter what you dream.

clouds ingest the moon.

raindrops die with a
splat on concrete causeways.

the floodgates are about to burst.

a banshee howls
over our love.

Forty-eight:
Sleep Patterns May Change

- Changes in sleep patterns—how long you sleep or when you sleep—are common while healing.

- If you have trouble falling asleep, wake up repeatedly during the night or wake up too early, this is known as *insomnia*.

- Above all, insomnia is nothing to worry about. In fact, worrying about not sleeping can cause one to lose sleep. We all don't "need" eight hours every night, so if you are sleeping less for a while, that's fine.

- You might try a glass of warm, low-fat milk before going to bed. Listen to soothing music, or to a tape of an uplifting meditation or lecture. If you find yourself *trying* to go to sleep for more than an hour, get up and do something else for a while. This breaks the pattern of worrying about worrying about sleeping.

- If you wake at night, read or listen to something comforting and inspiring. Or, you might try meditation, contemplation or prayer. Late at night, when everything is still, is a wonderful time for contacting the goodness within and around you.

- Over-the-counter sleeping pills are *not* recommended.

- If you fear your insomnia is severe, see your doctor.

- On the other hand, you may find yourself sleeping "too much." There is no such thing as "too much" sleep after a loss. Sleep until you wake up. Nap when you want to. Consider it part of your overall healing.

Someday I will
categorize
the
circle of pain
I put myself through
every time I get
hung up in someone.

I'll have a lot of time
to do it, too.

The insomnia's beginning.

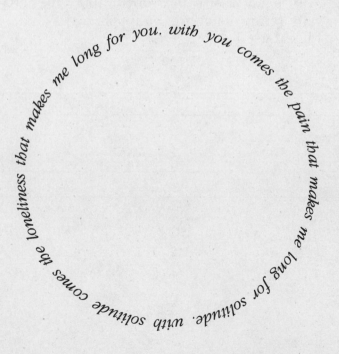

with you comes the pain that makes me long for solitude. with solitude comes the loneliness that makes me long for you.

Forty-nine:
Sexual Desire May Change

- A decrease—or complete lack—of sexual desire is often experienced after a loss. It is nothing to worry about. The body needs its energy for healing, and it automatically channels all available energy to that purpose.

- Also common after loss is difficulty—or inability—to perform sexually. While frustrating and sometimes embarrassing, this, too, is nothing to worry about. Now is not the time to put more pressure on yourself. It's OK to take a break from sex for a while.

- Full sexual desire and functioning will naturally return when the body has had a chance to heal itself.

who took the
L out of
Lover?

Fifty:
Remaining Distraught Is
No Proof of Love

- Remaining distraught for a long period of time is not proof that you "really loved."

- *Of course* you really loved. If you hadn't, you wouldn't have felt the loss in the first place.

- The fact that you can heal rapidly is proof that you are focusing your energies on healing, not that you didn't love fully or completely.

- You are not duty-bound to feel pain any longer than it's actually there.

*I am missing you
far better than
I ever loved you.*

Fifty-one:
Surround Yourself with Goodness and Light

- Whenever you think of it, ask that you be surrounded by all the Goodness and Light you can imagine.

- "Good" is such an obvious thing, it's difficult to define. We all know what we consider the best, the highest, the greatest, the goodest. You can think of "Good" as in "The Good Earth," or "Good" as "God" with an extra "o!" added.

- Light is a concept that seems to permeate almost every religious belief and spiritual practice. The Light of Nature to the Light of the Holy Spirit; the Light of the Sun to the Light of the Son.

- Whenever you call upon this Goodness and Light, it's a good idea to ask that it do its work for your highest good and the highest good of all concerned. In this way, our own personal preferences of the moment are not competing with whatever higher good may be planned for us.

- Breathe deeply of Goodness and Light. Let it fill every cell of your body. Breathe it into any areas (mental, emotional or physical) in need of healing.

- Asking for Goodness and Light to surround, fill, protect and heal you, for your highest good and the highest good of all concerned, need not take long—a few seconds at most (as long as it took you to read this sentence).

- It takes so little time, and the potential rewards are so great, we consider it a good investment in your healing and growing.

*Life is
not a
struggle.*

*It's a
wiggle.*

Fifty-two:
Pray, Meditate, Contemplate

- Whatever methods of prayer, meditation or contemplation you know—or would like to know better—now is a good time to use them.

- When we become still, the pain may resurface. That's fine. Let it be there, and continue with your inner work. Hurt that arises during prayer, meditation or contemplation is healing in nature.

- When praying, we suggest you ask, primarily, for the strength to endure, the power to heal and the wisdom to learn.

I missed you last night.
I missed you this morning.
I meditated.
I no longer miss you.
I love you.

Fifty-three:
Keep a Journal

- You might find keeping a journal or diary helpful.

- Putting your thoughts and emotions on paper is a good way of getting things out, of setting them in order.

- Don't add any "I will make an entry every day or else" rules to your journal keeping. Write when you feel like it, and when you don't, forget it.

- (The various authors of this tome have, at one time or another, attempted to keep journals. Only one of us [the compulsive one] thus far has succeeded for more than a month.)

I write only
until I cry,
which is why
so few poems
this month
have been
completed.

It's just
that
I

Fifty-four:
There Is a Beauty in Sadness

- There is a certain beauty in sadness (and here we mean genuine sadness, *not* self-pity).

- We cannot elaborate upon this further (not even the corn-fed poet in our midst dares do that), but we thought it was worth mentioning. If you are *enjoying* the beauty of being sad, it's perfectly all right.

you left
traces
of your self
all over my room:

a poem scribbled in the
margin of a book.

a corner of a page
turned over in another book.

your smell on my blanket.

where are you tonight?

in whose room are you leaving
traces?

are you perhaps
discovering
the traces of my self
I left on your soul?

Fifty-five:
Let Yourself Heal Fully

- Let the healing process run its full course.

- A time of convalescence is very important.

- For a while, don't become involved in an all-consuming passionate romance or a new project that requires great time and energy.

- Just follow your daily routine—and let yourself heal.

- If you do not allow the hurt to heal completely, you may find emotional over-sensitivity the result. You might flinch at every new encounter.

- Let yourself heal.

It will never be the same.
I will never be the same.

You came.
We loved.
You left.

I will survive until I survive.

And one day, I will
find
myself alive again.

And another day,
another's path will
run parallel to mine
—for awhile.

And yet another day,
you will return,
and I will see

It is not the same.

Fifty-six:
Affirm Yourself

- To "affirm" is to "make firm." Make firm the loving, healing and positive thoughts you have about yourself and your life.

- An affirmation usually begins "I am..." and is always stated in the present tense. Claim what you want as though you already have it. *"I am* healthy, wealthy and happy," not *"I want to be* healthy, wealthy and happy."

- Say aloud—over and over—these, or any other affirmations you may create:

  —"I am alive. I will survive."

  —"I am healing."

  —"I am surrendering to the process of healing."

  —"I am healing fully."

  —"I am healing naturally."

  —"I am gentle with myself."

  —"My heart is mending."

  —"I am stronger."

  —"I have the courage to grow."

  —"I am grateful for so much."

  —"I am patient with my healing."

  —"My patience will outlast my pain."

*I am
the nicest
thing I could
ever do for
myself.*

Fifty-seven:
Visualization

- Visualizing is imagining the outcome of something—what the future will be.

- We all visualize—often. We consider the future, and envision it either positively or negatively. Our problem occurs when we *negatively* visualize—imagining a future of lack, loneliness and despair.

- Take a moment and visualize a *positive* outcome. Imagine yourself healed, happily alive, thriving, loving and loved.

- Use as many of your senses as you can. See, feel, hear, taste and smell your joyful, nurturing future.

- Start slowly—a minute or so at first. Then build—visualization by visualization, day by day—imagining your positive future for longer and longer periods of time.

- Soon, your present will be the positive future you imagine now. That—or something greater, of course—for your highest good and the highest good of all concerned.

When we are
together
we are
one,

when we are
apart
each is
whole.

Let this be our dream.
Let this be our goal.

Fifty-eight:
Use Color to Lift Your Spirit

- You've probably noticed that certain colors have certain effects. We feel different walking into a dimly lit black room than we do walking into a brightly lit yellow room.

- As much as possible, stay in the "up" spectrum of colors—yellow, orange, red and pastels.

- Also, surround yourself with green—be it clothing, food, furniture or plants. Green is soothing and seems to promote healing and growth.

- And stay away from black and blue—you've been bruised enough already.

*Color
me
healed.*

Fifty-nine:
Laugh!

- Laughter is one of the most healing activities around.

- Whatever it is that makes you laugh, do it.

- Rent a video, buy a comedy tape, read a funny book, talk to people who make you laugh. Ask your friends to call you with anecdotes, stories and jokes they may have, hear or meet.

- And, yes, it's OK to laugh about your loss.

- There is a fine line between tragedy and comedy. Seeing the humor in your loss, your reaction to the loss and even your memories about what was lost, can be healing.

- You are not being disloyal to that which you loved by seeing the humor in him, her or it.

- Humor can, in fact, honor the relationship.

Why must I
always fall for

chicken shits
on
ego trips?

Sixty:
As Healing Continues...

* As your healing continues, you will find

    —your thinking sharpened

    —your judgement sounder and more reliable

    —your concentration and memory improved

    —a desire to be with others more

    —a desire to do more for others

    —your feelings become more expansive, optimistic and alive

* You'll feel stronger, more content and independent.

* You'll want to get out, get moving and try new things.

A new morning
of a
new life
without you.

So?

There will be others.
much finer,
much mine-er.

And until then,
there is me.

And because I treated
you
well,
I like me better.

Also, the sun rises.

GROWING

and
through
all the tears
and the
sadness
and the
pain
comes the
one thought
that can
make
me internally
smile again:

I
have
loved.

Sixty-one:
You're Stronger Now

- You have experienced a loss, encountered it with courage (at least *some* of the time) and have survived.

- You've learned that

    —You can survive.

    —The pain does lessen.

    —Much of what you feared did *not* come to pass.

    —Healing does occur.

- But don't just settle for surviving and healing. Use this experience as a springboard for greater growth.

the last day of my
loving you is
at hand.

in hand,
a pen, writing one of
the last poems
exclusively yours.

my pain fades,
as autumn did.

winter is too intense
a season to miss
someone in.

the last leaf
fell today.

the first snow
falls tonight.

Sixty-two:
Let Go of the Loss and Move On

- At a certain point (and that point differs from loss to loss and from person to person), it's time to leave the loss behind and move on.

- Don't be surprised if you actually miss the process of mourning. Some people mourn the loss of the mourning process.

- Let go of the past. Look forward to the future.

- You will, of course, occasionally look over your shoulder, but, for the most part, focus on the future and keep moving ahead.

- Let yourself enjoy the excitement of uncertainty.

I shall miss loving you.

*I shall miss the
Comfort
of your embrace.*

*I shall miss the
Loneliness
of waiting for your
calls that never came.*

*I shall miss the Joy
of our comings,
and Pain
of your goings.*

*and,
after a time,
I shall miss*

*missing
loving
you.*

Sixty-three:
Forgiveness Is Letting Go

- To forgive does not just mean to pardon, it means to let go.

- Jesus, probably the greatest teacher of forgiveness in history ("Forgive them, Father, for they know not what they do"), used the Aramaic word *shaw* when he spoke of forgiveness. *Shaw* means "to untie."

- If you are tied to a rock that is pulling you down in the water, all you have to do is *forgive it* (untie it) and swim toward the light.

- When you forgive the past, you untie yourself from the past, and are free.

- To forgive also means to be *for* (in favor of) *giving* (to deliver a gift). When you forgive, you affirm that you are in favor of giving.

- To whom do you give? Another? Sometimes. Yourself? Always. When you release another to go his or her own way, you free yourself to do the same.

- The process of giving yourself this gift of freedom is forgiveness.

*The forgetting
is difficult.*

*The remembering,
worse.*

Sixty-four:
Forgive the Other Person

- Whenever you can, as soon as you can, forgive the other person.

- You do this not for the other person, you do this for yourself—your peace of mind and the quality of your future relationships.

- A simple, but remarkably effective, technique of forgiveness was taught by John-Roger. (It's a good idea to surround yourself with Goodness and Light before beginning this process.)

- First say, "I forgive _____ (the person, event or thing that caused your loss) for _____ (what they did to cause the loss)." That's the first part of forgiveness.

- Then say, "I forgive myself for judging _____ (same person, event or thing) for _____ (same transgression)."

- The second part of forgiveness—forgiving yourself for judging another—is important, but often overlooked. Your *judgement* of the other person's action is what hurt you emotionally. When you forgive his or her action, you must also forgive *your judgement* of his or her action.

- It may take many repetitions of the above sentences to untie the many layers of transgressions and judgements—but keep at it. You can, and will, be free.

The love
I give you
is second hand.

I feel it first.

Sixty-five:
Forgive Yourself

- Whenever you can, as soon as you can, forgive yourself.

- Whatever errors, transgressions, failings, weaknesses, infractions or mistakes you feel you made to cause the loss—real or imagined—forgive yourself for those.

- The process is the same as forgiving another. Surround yourself with Goodness and Light and say, "I forgive myself for _____ (the failing)." Then add, "I forgive myself for judging myself for _____ (the same failing)."

- Again, the most powerful part of the process is forgiving yourself for having judged yourself for whatever you did (or didn't do). Who (besides parents, teachers, society and nearly everyone else) said you must be perfect?

- As John-Roger pointed out, "We're not perfect. We're human."

- Forgive yourself for being human, forgive yourself for judging your humanness, and move on.

- A great book on forgiving yourself is *Making Peace with Yourself* by Harold H. Bloomfield, M.D. with Leonard Felder, Ph.D. You can find it at your local bookstore.

At a critical moment I said:

I would rather you go
and regret your going
than stay
and regret your staying.

Some day I'm going to
learn to keep my mouth
shut.

Sixty-six:
Take Stock of the Good

• Now that the pain is less, understanding can grow.

• You may begin seeing change and separation as a natural, inevitable and necessary part of life.

• The relationship brought you a great deal of good (that's why you missed it so terribly when it was no longer there). Much of it is still with you. Now is the time to take stock of that good:

>   —He taught you to appreciate good food.

>   —She occasioned your interest in skiing.

>   —That job taught you a great deal about computers.

• You are a better person for having loved.

Sifting through the
ashes of our relationship,

I find many things
to be grateful for.

I can say "thank you" for
warm mornings,
cold protein drinks,
and all the love you have ever offered
another.

I can say "thank you"
for being there,
willing to be shared.

I can say "thank you" for
the countless poems you were
the inspiration for and the
many changes you were
catalyst to.

But how, in my grasp of
the English language,
faltering as it is,
can I ever

thank you
for
Beethoven
?

Sixty-seven:
You Are a Better Person for Having Loved

- You cared.

- You became involved.

- You learned to invest yourself.

- Your interaction permitted loving and caring.

- Even though you lost, you are a better person for having loved.

You were the best of loves,
you were the worst of loves...

and you left behind several
unintended gifts:

Through you I re-examined my
need (uh, desire?) for one significant
other to share my life.

You commanded in me an unwilling
(but probably much-needed)
re-evaluation of self, behavior patterns,
relationshipping, & a corresponding
change in attitudes;
i.e. growth.

I'm nicer to people.

I'm more in touch with my feelings,
the things and persons around me, life.

And, of course, a scattering of poems
(the best of poems, the worst of poems)
that never would have happened
without your disruptions.

Thanks.

Sixty-eight:
Praise Yourself for the
Courage to Relate

- You are a richer, deeper, wiser person for having invested in a relationship—even if that relationship ended in loss.

- Praise yourself for the courage to relate.

- "Courage" is based on the French word for "from the heart." It took great heart to care, to be vulnerable, to love. Praise, honor and celebrate your heart.

- Would we dare quote something as clichéd as, "It is far, far better to have loved and lost than never to have loved at all"? Of course we wouldn't.

- Now's the time to see what lessons you learned from your loss, and what possible good is contained within the loss.

Love,
no matter what
you feel it for,
is still love.

The object does not
change the emotion.

But the emotion
quite often
changes the object.

Sixty-nine:
Changes

- A new chapter in your life has begun, and is by now well under way.

- Know that you have the ability to make the changes this new chapter requires.

- Be prepared to make an adjustment, perhaps two or three.

- Now is a good time to start experimenting with new behaviors, new activities, new ways of fulfilling the day-to-day needs that are still unattended.

- It will take courage, but it is exciting.

- This might even be fun!

The need you
grew
still remains.

But less and less
you seem the way
to fill that need.

I am.

Seventy:
Start Anew

- Be open.

- Be open to new people, places, ideas, experiences.

- It's time to move far beyond the "I'll never love again—love only brings pain" attitude.

- Do your best to

    —Remain trusting.

    —Maintain a lively curiosity.

    —Be open to learn.

- Visit new places.

- Now's the time to

    —Redecorate (or at least clean) your apartment.

    —Buy (or make) some new clothes.

    —Learn—whatever it is you've always wanted to know (pottery or politics).

- Choose (and pursue) new goals.

The difference between
love and loving

is the difference between
fish and fishing.

Seventy-one:
Invite New People into Your Life

- Now is the time to make new friends, associates, colleagues.

- Attend meetings, concerts, plays, social events—any public gathering of kindred souls. (It's fine to go alone.)

- Meet your neighbors.

- Find in yourself the courage to introduce yourself to anyone—even a total stranger.

- When making new acquaintances, ask questions that require more than a "yes" or "no" answer.

- Use "how" and "why" questions rather than only "what" or "who."

- Offer to drive people home or invite them out for a cup of coffee.

- Carry paper and pen to share phone numbers. You might even have calling cards printed. (Whatever happened to calling cards?)

I am not
a total
stranger.

I am a
perfect
stranger.

Seventy-two:
Develop New Interests...

- Now's the time to develop new interests.

- Archery's always held some fascination? How about water polo? Marco Polo? Piano solo? Explore whatever or wherever you want to explore—on video or in person.

- Is it time to get that personal computer?

- A new language? Brush up on an old language? (English, perhaps?) How about a course in bookkeeping—or bee keeping?

- Gardening? Sewing? Canning? Auto maintenance? Garment weaving? Gourmet cooking? Metal shop?

- Read a book. Take a class. Learn—and above all *do*—something new.

- Yes, we can even recommend a book on computers! It's Peter McWilliams' *Personal Computer Book* and it's available at local bookstores, or by calling 1-800-LIFE-101.

Seventy-three:
...But Don't Forget
the Old Interests

- Don't forget about the old interests and activities you've let lapse.

- Rediscover the ones that gave you a special sense of achievement, excitement, joy.

- In choosing new and old interests, be sure to intersperse those activities which require people and those which you do best alone.

Seventy-four:
Groups

- Perhaps you feel shy, or simply don't want to make new contacts on your own. If so, groups may be the answer.

- There are literally hundreds of groups you can join. Check the Yellow Pages under "Clubs," "Associations," "Fellowships," etc. You can join a group to learn something, to travel, to meet people, to celebrate common interests—there are so many possibilities.

- Church-sponsored groups are readily available.

- There are many groups that cater especially to the newly-single-again individual. They include

  —Parents without Partners

  —The Singletons

  —Singles Dating Club

  —Over-30 Club

- The Toastmasters' Club helps develop speaking skills that may be helpful in expressing yourself to others.

- Adult education classes, "Y" groups, and programs sponsored by The American Youth Hostels offer opportunities not only for learning new skills, but for meeting others in a comfortable environment.

Someday we are going to be lovers.
Maybe married.
At the very least, an affair.

What's your name?

Seventy-five:
Self-Improvement Anyone?

- It may be time to change (one at a time, please) something you'd like to change about yourself:

  —Go on a diet.

  —Stop smoking.

  —Stop drinking.

  —Begin an exercise program.

  Seek professional help if necessary, and/or join a recognized group (AA, Weight Watchers, etc.). Be gentle with yourself, but set a realistic goal and then achieve it.

- At the same time, accentuate your positives. Be even more

  —tolerant

  —trusting/trustworthy

  —helpful

  —giving

  —concerned

  —loving

  —yourself

- A great book to read is *LIFE 101: Everything We Wish We Had Learned About Life in School—But Didn't* by John-Roger and Peter McWilliams. Available at your local bookstore, or by calling 1-800-LIFE-101.

Maturity
is a very
magical
thing...

Now you see it,
now you don't.

Seventy-six:
Your Words Have Power

- You should not use "should."

- Never use "never."

- We wish you wouldn't use "wish."

- Hopefully you'll give up "hope."

- Maybe you'd be better off without "maybe."

- You must not use "must."

- Things are seldom black or white. We live in a world of "often," "sometimes" and "seldom." Using those words gives those around you more freedom—more freedom to be themselves, to be human and simply to be.

- And be sure to give the same freedom to yourself.

*I've heard a lot
about the dangers of
living beyond one's means.*

*What worries me, however,
is my current habit of
living beyond my meanings.*

Seventy-seven:
Think "Both/And" Rather Than "Either/Or"

- Your relationship with whomever or whatever you loved was both "good" and "bad." Such is life.

- Life is not *either* good *or* bad. Life includes *both* good *and* bad.

- Life is not lived in one extreme, struggling to eliminate the other. Life is the continuum between the extremes.

- After a loss, people tend to dwell on the darker side of life and long for a time when everything will be "perfect" again.

- Life was never perfect. Life always included *both* perfect *and* imperfect. It always has, and it always will.

- Welcome to life.

Perfect joy and
perfect sorrow.

One following another,
following another.

The poles—the extremes—
of emotional life, and
all points in between.

Following one another.
Following one another.

Gently up, gently down,
like the ocean under a boat.

Seventy-eight:
The Freedom to Choose

- Enjoy your freedom.

- You're in control now.

- Make the most of the ability to choose

    —where
    —what
    —how
    —when
    —why
    —who

- You can make (and make well) the necessary decisions to

    —sort
    —clean
    —rearrange
    —discard
    —acquire

- You are bringing order into your world again. You can choose the world you want to have around you.

- A great book on choosing goals and fulfilling dreams is *DO IT! Let's Get Off Our Buts* by John-Roger and Peter McWilliams. Available (guess where!) at your local bookstore, or by calling 1-800-LIFE-101.

*I don't want
to build my
life around
you,*

*but I do want to
include you
in the building
of my life.*

Seventy-nine:
It's OK to Ask

- Seek the support of others in achieving your goals.

- Do not, however, depend upon their approval or assistance before you move toward your goal.

- If they don't want to go to Hawaii with you, aloha alone.

It is a risk to love.

What if it doesn't
work out?

Ah,
but what if it does?

Eighty:
It's OK for Others to Say No

- Rejection isn't personal.

- When people say "no" to you, they're merely saying "yes" to some other portion of *their* life. *You* have nothing to do with it. Therefore, there's no need to take it personally.

- When you learn to allow others to say "no" and not become upset by it, you get two rewards: (1) you are less upset, and (2) you tend to ask others more often for what you want. (If you don't experience "no" as a rejection, then there's no fear of rejection.)

- The more people you ask, the more chances you have of getting what you want.

- In baseball, the very best hitters only get three hits every ten times at bat. And guess who has the all-time strike-out record? Babe Ruth.

- If one-third the people you ask say yes, you are doing very well. Even if only one in 100 says yes, that's one more than you would have had without asking.

*I don't know
how to lose.*

That's part of the problem.

*I don't know
how to win, either.*

That's the other part.

Eighty-one:
It's OK for Others to Say Yes

- Some people fear acceptance more than rejection.

- This usually springs from a lack of self worth. When we don't feel worthy, we think things like, "You'll go out with me? I thought you had good taste," or ask questions such as, "I'm hired? What's wrong with the company?"

- The secret of self-esteem is to do good things, *and remember that you've done them.*

- Learn to accept acceptance.

- When people say "You look lovely," "That was beautiful," "I appreciate your skill," "You make me feel great," take it in.

help me.

show me that
I can love with
<u>*out*</u>
fears, frustrations,
falsehoods, hesitations.

show me the
face of
god.

Eighty-two:
Fear Can Be a Friend

- When we label an emotion "fear," we tend to back away from the action causing the fear (basically, anything new).

- If we label the same emotion "excitement" or "adventure," we have the energy to move into the new activity with renewed vigor and enthusiasm.

- Fear is the energy to do your best in a new situation.

- There is no need to "get rid of" fear. We need only reprogram our *attitude* toward fear. If we treat it as a friend, it makes a great companion on our explorations of the new.

The world is good.

I feel whole & directed.

Touch my Joy with me.

*I cannot keep
my smiles
in single file.*

Eighty-three:
The Antidote for Anxiety
Is Action

• Worried about something?

• *Do something* about it.

• Take a *physical action* to correct, solve, com-
municate or educate yourself about whatever
concerns you.

• The action may be as simple as a phone call,
writing a letter, taking a walk or reading a
book.

• You may discover there is nothing to worry
about. If you discover there *is* something to
worry about, use worry as the energy to
make an improvement.

We are such
good friends
you & I.

After being
with you
for only
a little while

I
no longer
relate to
sadness.

Eighty-four:
Postpone Procrastination

- We're going to write this chapter real soon.
- Honest.
- We promise.
- Cross our hearts.
- Tomorrow.
- Thursday at the *latest*.

I have this
great poem on
procrastination—

I'll send it to you
real soon.

As soon as
I write it
down.

Eighty-five:
The Past

- Remember: the healing process continues even while you're growing.

- Memories may come drifting back one Sunday morning or when "our song" is played on the radio.

- Expect this. It doesn't mean you're sinking back into depression, it's just the ebb and flow of healing and growing.

- Be with the feeling. Know that it soon will pass.

I know our
time together
is no more.

Then why do
words
come to mind
that call you
back?

Why do I plan
lifetimes
that include
you?

Why do I
torture
myself
with love
I never felt
while you were
here?

Eighty-six:
Anniversaries

- You may experience the loss in miniature when anniversaries, birthdays or other significant reminders appear.

- Know that your recovery from the pain of such reminders will be faster, and that all you've learned to survive, heal and grow the first time around will be just as valuable the second time.

- The third anniversary will hurt less; the fourth, even less.

- Note the dates of upcoming anniversaries. Plan activities that are particularly enjoyable, uplifting and comforting on those days.

- Eventually, all you'll remember is the loving.

It's been two years
since we talked last.

You lead a church choir
somewhere.

The pauses between your
sentences are longer.
More pregnant—or so
you would like the world
to believe. They make me
as uncomfortable as
ever.

"A person out of the past"
you keep saying, unwilling
to accept my present.

Questions answered by questions.
Statements questioned by silence.

Your ambiguity and my ambivalence
clash again,
for the last time.

Eighty-seven:
Solitude

- You can enjoy being alone again.
- Explore and appreciate solitude.
- "Alone" does not mean "lonely."
- Solitary pursuits can be
    - —delight-filled
    - —restful
    - —exciting
    - —in joy able
    - —a prelude to creativity
    - —spending time with the most important person in your life—you
    - —fun
- Enjoying yourself is a prerequisite to genuinely enjoying others.

The difference between
"a1one"
and
"a11 one"
is
1
(me),

and a little space.

Eighty-eight:
Creativity

- You'll find yourself once again remarkably in touch with your creative energy. Do something with it.

- What do you do that is creative? Write? Sing? Dance? Act? Bake cherry pies? Give massages?

- Well, whatever it is or they are, *DO!*

- For example, did you know that you are a poet? Prove it to yourself. Sit down with a pencil and paper. (Pen and paper will do.) Find out what you're feeling, find a thought or group of words that fits that feeling and write them down.

Now, instead of writing the words this way,

write
them
this way.

Put words that you want to
stand
out
on separate lines.
Forget
every
thing
"they" taught you about
poetry
in
school.

Do this three or four times. Keep it up. You'll get a poem. Honest.

Rule 1: Line for line, poetry need not rhyme.

Rule 2: Honest, clear expression of a fully felt experience is what poetry is all about.

Eighty-nine:
Enjoy!

- Be happy, cheerful, joyful, delighted, pleased—as often as you can, as much as you can, for as long as you can.

- You may feel some guilt about being joyful after a loss. Know that you are not being disloyal to the love you lost by moving on with your life—and moving on must certainly include joy.

This poem
is a kiss
for your mind.

Ninety:
Appreciation

- As you grow, you will begin to regain your sense of appreciation, of awe. The sense of childlike wonder, which was lost to you for a while, will return.

- Enjoy it.

- Sunsets and children laughing. City streets and country roads. The wonder of "this time called life."

- The Wonder Years need never end.

The cosmic dance
to celestial melodies,

free form within
patterns of precise
limitations.

The painting I know
so well. The canvas
I want to learn,

and, perhaps,
someday,
the artist.

Ninety-one:
Do Something for
Someone Else

- If you begin feeling sorry for yourself (not genuine sorrow, but the "poor put-upon me" variety), the best way to cure this is to do something for someone else.

> —Drive someone to the grocery store.
>
> —Tune a friend's car.
>
> —Volunteer to take calls at the local suicide prevention center, rap line, hot line or similar service.
>
> —Visit someone in a hospital—anyone.
>
> —Wash windows or do housework for an older person.
>
> —Read to the blind.
>
> —Talk to the lonely.
>
> —Listen to the ignored.

- Giving is the greatest gift you can give yourself.

- As the saying goes, "Don't return a favor; pass it on." Now's the time to pass on all the good favors you received during your time of loss.

In taking,
I get.

In giving,
I receive.

In being loved,
I am filled full.

In loving,
I am fulfilled.

The greatest gift
is to fill a need
unnoticed.

Ninety-two:
Appreciate Your Growth

- Having weathered a crisis, expect to discover
  - —a stronger you
  - —a different you
  - —a more evolved you
- You're changing and growing into
  - —a happier you
  - —a more joyful you
  - —an independent you

The world outside
is a mirror,
reflecting the

good & bad
joy & sorrow
laughter & tears

within me.

Some people are
difficult mirrors
to look into,

but you...

I look at you
and I see
all the beauty
inside of me.

Ninety-three:
Your Happiness Is Up to You

- Happiness depends on your *attitude* toward what happens to you, not on what happens to you.

- It may sound revolutionary, but problems don't have to make you unhappy.

- This runs counter to our cultural programming—which tells us we *must* react in certain negative ways to certain "negative" events.

- Nonetheless, happiness is always *our choice.* That is a reality of life.

- Stop waiting for Prince Charming, Cinderella, more money, the right job, total health *or anything else* before you're happy.

- Stop waiting.

- Choose satisfaction.

- Be happy.

- Now.

I am worthy.

*I am worthy of my life and
all the good that is in it.*

*I am worthy of
my friends and their friendship.*

*I am worthy of spacious skies, amber waves
of grain and purple mountain majesties
above the fruited plain. (I am worthy, too,
of the fruited plain.)*

*I am worthy of a degree of happiness
that could only be referred to as
"sinful" in less enlightened times.*

*I am worthy of creativity,
sensitivity and appreciation.*

*I am worthy of peace of mind, peace on Earth,
peace in the valley and a piece of the action.*

I am worthy of God's presence in my life.

*I am worthy
of my love.*

Ninety-four:
Celebrate!

- Throw a Survival Celebration party.

- Invite everyone who helped in your survival, healing and growth. Ask each of them to bring a friend (a great way to meet new people).

- If a party is not your style, be sure to acknowledge the help and support you received from others. Send thank-you notes, flowers, gifts or whatever you find appropriate.

- Remember the value of the help you received when you come across others in need.

- And, especially, give yourself a pat on the back for a job well done.

- You've been through losing, surviving, healing and growing.

- Now it's time for celebrating.

CONGRATULATIONS!

My love and
God's Light
be with you

in all that
you are and
in all that
you do.

A companion workbook to
How to Survive the Loss of a Love
is available.
It's entitled

Surviving, Healing & Growing

❦

How to Survive the Loss of a Love
is available on audio tape
—complete and unabridged.

❦

The poetry in this volume was taken from

Come Love with Me & Be My Life:
The Collected Romantic Poetry
of Peter McWilliams

❦

Available at your local bookstore,
or by calling

1-800-LIFE-101

or you can write to

Prelude Press
8165 Mannix Drive
Los Angeles, California 90046

THANK YOU!

About the Authors

MELBA COLGROVE, Ph.D. earned degrees in literature, foreign trade, special education, counseling and organizational psychology. She received her Ph.D. in 1966 from the University of Michigan, having written her doctoral dissertation on creative problem solving. Presently, she is writing and consulting from her home in Oxford, Michigan. She is also on the staff of *Waterford Family Counseling* in Waterford, Michigan.

HAROLD H. BLOOMFIELD, M.D. is one of the leading psychological educators of our time. A Yale-trained psychiatrist, Dr. Bloomfield introduced meditation, holistic health and family peacemaking to millions of people. He is an Adjunct Professor of Psychology at Union Graduate School. A book he co-authored on meditation was on the *New York Times* bestseller list for over six months. Dr. Bloomfield is co-author of other bestsellers including *Making Peace with Your Parents, Making Peace with Yourself, Inner Joy* and *Lifemates*. His books have sold over 5,000,000 copies in twenty-two languages. Dr. Bloomfield is among the most sought-after keynote speakers and seminar leaders in the world. He is a frequent guest on the *Oprah Winfrey Show, Donahue, Sally Jesse Raphael* and *CNN.* His articles appear in such magazines as *Cosmopolitan, Ladies Home Journal, Health* and *New Woman.* Dr. Bloomfield is in the private practice of psychiatry and psychotherapy in Del Mar, California.

PETER McWILLIAMS published his first book, a collection of poetry, at the age of seventeen. His series of poetry books went on to sell more than 3,500,000 copies. A volume of his poetry and advice, *Surviving the Loss of a Love,* was the inspiration for this book. A book he co-authored on meditation was #1 on the *New York Times* bestseller list. His *The Personal Computer Book* was a bestseller. His *LIFE 101 Series* of books with John-Roger were all bestsellers. *(DO IT!* was #1 on the *New York Times* hardcover list.) He is a nationally syndicated columnist, teaches seminars, and has appeared on the *Oprah Winfrey Show, Donahue, Larry King* and *The Today Show.*